Dedicated To:
David & Camryn Figueroa
May 25, 2024

Written By: Abigail Gartland

Hello, my name is St. Cecilia!

I was born in Italy in the 200s!

That means, I was not born a Christian, but I fell in love with Jesus and followed his teachings.

When I grew up, I married a nice man.

My husband also loved Jesus, and he converted to Christianity, too!

During our prayer, an angel visited us.

The angel had two crowns!

One crown was made of roses...

The other was made of lilies!

We spent the rest of our lives teaching people about Jesus and helping them convert to Christianity.

I also love to give glory to God through music.

Do you want to be more like me?

You can celebrate my feast day with me on November 22nd.

I am the patron saint of music!

Ask God to be with you when you sing at Mass.

I pray for you every day of your life.

St. Cecilia, Pray for Us

Copyright:

Clipart: © PentoolPixie © LimeandKiwiDesigns
Licensed purchased: 1/10/2024

About the Author

Abigail Gartland

I love the saints and I love my faith. The idea for sharing the stories of the saints with little ones came when my dear friends were expecting their first baby. I wanted to create something as unique and special as our friendship. Each book is dedicated to very special people and groups who have enriched my faith in different ways. I am blessed to write these stories and appreciate the unending support of my family and friends. When I am not writing, am a middle school teacher. I hope you enjoy these stories. I pray for each and every person who opens one of my books to learn more about the saints.

Abbie